Contents

KU-739-736

Battles and wars

Why war?

Throughout history, wars have been fought because rulers wanted to increase their power and wealth by taking over lands, people or trade controlled by others – or because they were forced to defend their own lands, people or trade from an enemy.

Sometimes wars were fought to spread a new religion. Even when a war was being fought for profit, leaders often used religion to make it appear that they were fighting for noble reasons.

A war can involve one or many battles. It may end only when one side finally loses the will to go on or has no army left. Or it may end after a single, decisive fight. The Hundred Years War of 1337–1453 is an example of the first kind of war. The Norman **invasion** of England in 1066 is an example of the second kind of war.

Agincourt 1415

From 1337 onwards, English kings repeatedly invaded France, claiming to be its rightful ruler. In 1415, Henry V's army found its way back to England cut off at Agincourt by a French force five times as big. Against all odds, and with tiny losses, Henry won a brilliant victory and came home safely. At the time it seemed that the battle of Agincourt would be decisive. But the Hundred Years War went on until the French finally drove the English out in 1453, nearly 40 years later.

A French manuscript picture of Agincourt made 70 years after the event. Artists at that time did not try to make their pictures very realistic.

TURNING POINTS IN HISTORY

66

sive Battle

MES

Books should be returned or renewed by the last date stamped above

Awarded for excellence
to Arts & Libraries

Kent
County
Council

First published in Great Britain by Heinemann Library
Halley Court, Jordan Hill, Oxford OX2 8EJ
a division of Reed Educational & Professional Publishing Ltd.
Heinemann is a registered trademark of Reed Educational & Professional Publishing Ltd.

OXFORD FLORENCE PRAGUE MADRID ATHENS MELBOURNE AUCKLAND
KUALA LUMPUR SINGAPORE TOKYO IBADAN NAIROBI KAMPALA JOHANNESBURG
GABORONE PORTSMOUTH NH (USA) CHICAGO MEXICO CITY SAO PAOLO

Designed by Jim Evoy
Illustrations by Jeff Edwards, Oxford Illustrators
Printed in Hong Kong

03 02 01
10 9 8 7 6 5 4 3 2

ISBN 0 431 06877 1

This book is also available in hardback (ISBN 0 431 06876 3).

British Library Cataloguing in Publication Data
Tames, Richard, 1946–
1066: a decisive battle. - (Turning points in history)
1.Hastings, Battle of, 1066 - Juvenile literature
I. Title II. Ten sixty six
942'.019.

Acknowledgements
The Publishers would like to thank the following for permission to reproduce photographs:
The Bridgeman Art Library, p.4; Dean and Chapter Library of Durham, p.24;
Dixon, C. M., p.10; e.t. archive, p.29 Holford, Michael, pp.5, 6, 8, 9, 12, 15, 16, 17, 18, 20, 25, 26, 27;
Public Record Office Image Library, p.28.

Cover photograph: The Bridgeman Art Library

Our thanks to Jane Shuter for her help in the preparation of this book.

Every effort has been made to contact copyright holders of any material reproduced in this book. Any
omissions will be rectified in subsequent printings if notice is given to the Publisher.

Some words are shown in bold, **like this**. You can find out what they mean
by looking in the glossary.

Hastings 1066

The battle of Hastings was decisive in both the short and the long term. It was fought between roughly equal forces of English and Normans, and might have gone either way. But when it ended, the English king lay dead and his army had fled.

The Normans were free to take over the country. Although there were rebellions, the invaders had come to stay. They took over the government, land and church, introducing new laws, customs and fashions. They even changed the language.

The Norman conquest was one of the most important turning points in English history. There have been many threats of **invasion** since, but 1066 was the last successful one. This is very different from Europe, where foreign conquest has repeatedly upset the life of many nations. France was last invaded in 1940.

Norman knights attack Anglo-Saxon spearmen on a small hill. One of the 72 scenes from the *Bayeux Tapestry* – a pictorial record of the invasion of England in 1066. Several scenes are shown throughout this book.

Who will be king?

What were the rules?

In theory, when an English king died, his eldest son succeeded to the throne. In practice, another son or male relative might take over if he was a better soldier, or had the support of powerful lords or foreign rulers, or was prepared to murder the obvious successor. Because the ruling families of England, Denmark and Normandy were mixed up with each other by marriage the situation could be even more uncertain and complicated.

Edgar's successors

The first ruler to be crowned king of all England was Edgar in 973. After his death in 975 England was ruled by Edgar's eldest son Edward, who was murdered in 978. Edward's brother Ethelred took over but was driven into **exile** by Danish invaders. Ethelred's son, Edmund, led an English fight back and divided England with the Danish king, Canute. After Edmund died in 1016, Canute became sole ruler of England, and later, of Denmark and Norway as well.

Harold is crowned King of England by the Archbishop of Canterbury, 1066. The figures on the left show him being offered the crown. Those on the right applaud his acceptance.

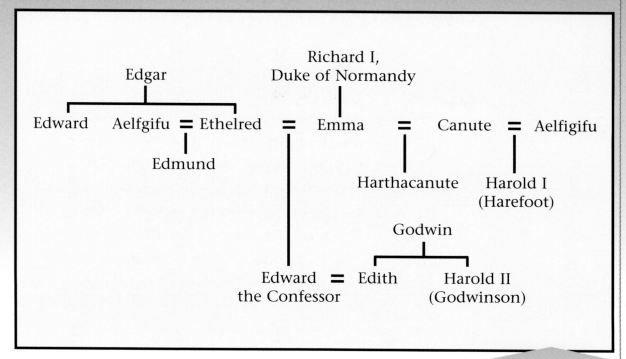

Family tree

After Canute

After Canute died in 1035, England was ruled by his sons, first by Harold Harefoot and then by his half-brother Harthacanute. Harthacanute had no children. In 1041, he brought his half-brother Edward back from exile in Normandy, where he had grown up. When Harthacanute died in 1042, Edward succeeded to the throne – despite a plot against him led by his own mother!

A very different kind of king

Canute and his sons were hard men, quite willing to use violence and **treachery** to defend their right to rule. Edward was very different. He was not warlike and was so religious he became known as 'The Confessor'. His main aim in life was to build a magnificent abbey at Westminster. He even moved his palace right next to it so that he could oversee all the details of the building.

Edward had been brought up in Normandy. His mother, Emma, was a Norman. He surrounded himself with Norman friends at court and gave them lands and important jobs in government. This made him unpopular with the English.

The reign of the Confessor

A meaningless marriage

The most powerful man in England was Godwin, earl of Wessex, who controlled most of the land in southern England. Edward the Confessor married Godwin's daughter, Edith, more to please Godwin than to please himself. Edward and Edith had no children. The **chroniclers** who later wrote the history of Edward's reign were monks. They said Edward wanted to live the holy life of a monk. It may be that Edith didn't want to have children with Edward. Or one of them might have had a medical problem which prevented it. Whatever the real reason, one thing was clear to everyone: Edward would have no son to succeed him.

A family quarrel

By 1049, Edward openly resented Godwin's power. In 1051, Edward took Godwin's lands away from him, sent him and his sons into exile and sent Edith to a **nunnery**.

The death of Edward the Confessor

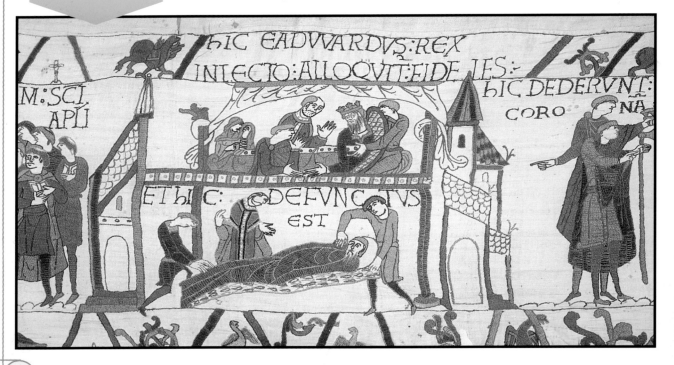

But Edward's Norman court became so unpopular that Godwin and his sons were able to gather an army of supporters. They forced Edward to give back their lands and send many of his Norman friends away. Godwin died in 1053 and his son, Harold Godwinson, then became the most powerful man in England.

The succession

Edward promised that after his death the English throne should pass to William, Duke of Normandy, to whom he was related through his mother, Emma. In 1064, Harold Godwinson travelled to Normandy, where he fought alongside William against the ruler of neighbouring Brittany.

William later claimed that Harold swore on holy relics that he agreed that William should succeed to the English throne. But when Edward the Confessor died in January 1066, Harold claimed that on his deathbed Edward had named him as his successor. Harold Godwinson therefore became king.

William collects supplies for his invasion fleet.

When he heard this, William of Normandy prepared an **invasion** fleet to take the English throne by force. Harold countered by stationing an army along the south coast and a fleet in the Channel to oppose him. By September, however, they had run out of supplies. The army was disbanded, the fleet sent back to London. The south lay unprotected – and then serious trouble began in the north.

Victories for Harold

My brother, my enemy

In 1063, Harold Godwinson's younger brother, Tostig, had helped him drive raiders back into Wales. But in 1065, Tostig's harsh rule as earl of Northumbria caused a local rebellion. Tostig was sent into **exile**. Harold did nothing to save him, thus turning him into a bitter enemy.

Raids foiled

In May 1066, Tostig returned with 60 ships and began raiding the English coast. He occupied the Kentish port of Sandwich, where he got more men and ships. When Harold sent forces against him he sailed to the island of Thanet, off Kent, joining up with another exile, Copsi. He had brought more ships from the Orkney Islands, which were under Norwegian control. Together they sailed up England's east coast, raiding Norfolk. At last earl Edwin of Mercia beat Tostig in a battle at Lindsey, Lincolnshire. Tostig, down to a dozen ships, fled north to Scotland.

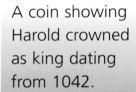

A coin showing Harold crowned as king dating from 1042.

Revenge sought

In September, Tostig returned south with King Harald Hardrada of Norway. Harald hoped to become ruler of England, just as Canute had been. Tostig and Harald had a large fleet of about 500 ships. They sailed up the Humber and Ouse and marched on York.

On 20 September, at Fulford Gate, in a bloody battle which cost both sides dearly, they defeated an English army led by Edwin of Mercia and his brother Morcar of Northumbria.

The invaders took York but camped outside it, some at Stamford Bridge, others at Riccall, where their ships were moored. Then they rested after their battle, gathering forces from the surrounding area before moving south against Harold Godwinson.

Surprise!

What Tostig and his allies did not know was that Harold was already racing north with a fresh army to confront them. On 25 September, he caught the invaders at Stamford Bridge. Some of them were west of the River Derwent, most of them were east of it and others were still at Riccall, where many had put their armour on board ship, ready to go south. The fighting was savage until Harald Hardrada fell, fatally wounded by an arrow through the throat. Reinforcements from Riccall then arrived, but exhausted by their forced march in armour, made little difference. After Tostig also fell, the invaders broke. Harold Godwinson let the survivors sail away. They needed just 20 ships.

Raiding and revenge – Harold catches up with Tostig

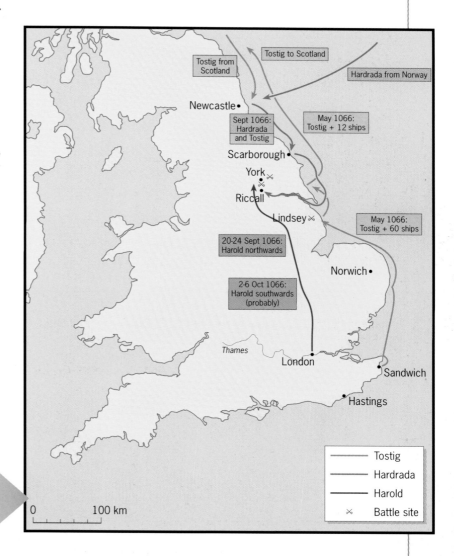

Tostig to Scotland

Tostig from Scotland

Hardrada from Norway

Newcastle

Sept 1066: Hardrada and Tostig

May 1066: Tostig + 12 ships

Scarborough

York

Riccall

Lindsey

May 1066: Tostig + 60 ships

20-24 Sept 1066: Harold northwards

Norwich

2-6 Oct 1066: Harold southwards (probably)

Thames

London

Sandwich

Hastings

	Tostig
	Hardrada
	Harold
✕	Battle site

0   100 km

A second challenge

South again!

Harold's victory finished off any further threat of Norwegian interference. But just one week later, on 1 October, he learned that William's Norman **invasion** fleet had landed in Sussex on 28 September. His earlier preparations for this invasion had fallen apart. Many of Harold's soldiers had been killed at Stamford Bridge. Most of the northern army had been killed in the fighting before he had arrived from the south. Harold rushed back to London with only his personal **bodyguard** of a few hundred men. He arrived on 6 October.

William's options

William had landed at Pevensey and was probably surprised that he was unopposed. He moved along the coast and set up a secure base camp at Hastings. He knew everything might hang on a single battle, so he cautiously decided against trying to capture London before Harold could get back from the north. Who knew what resistance he might meet in the woods on the way, or at London itself?

The Norman invasion fleet. William's boat had a figure of a trumpeter at the sternpost. Notice the horses on the other ships.

If he went inland, Harold could send the English fleet to the south coast to cut William off from ships with supplies and more soldiers from Normandy. So William decided to force Harold to come to him and fight where William wanted – in the open, where he could use his archers and **cavalry** to best advantage.

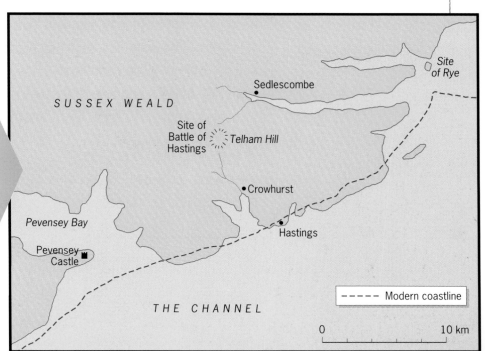

The Norman's landing site. The coastline was very different then. The sheltered lagoon at Pevensey no longer exists.

Harold's choice

Against all advice, Harold waited less than a week in London before heading south, raising soldiers in Kent and Sussex as he went. He could have waited longer to collect a much larger force from other parts of England. But Sussex was part of his family's lands and William's soldiers were attacking the local villages.

Harold may have hoped to keep William penned in around Hastings. Then he could starve William out. He may even have hoped to take the invaders completely by surprise, as he had surprised Harald and Tostig at Stamford Bridge. He ordered his men to gather on a ridge just outside Hastings. But William was warned by scouts of Harold's approach. It was William who moved first and came out to offer battle.

A kingdom lost and won

Taking position

On Saturday 14 October, 1066, William, Duke of Normandy, led an invading army along the road from Hastings towards London. 11 km from Hastings the army of Harold Godwinson, King of England, blocked the way. The English **infantry** held a ridge 1 km long, with their shields overlapped to make a defensive wall. William's troops drew up in three lines: archers to the front, followed by infantry, then **cavalry**.

The fight begins

William's archers began the attack. But they were firing uphill, so had little effect on the English, who were protected by their wall of shields. William's infantry then charged through a shower of spears, axes and stones thrown downhill at them. The two armies met and fought hand to hand. The English line held firm, so William sent in his cavalry. Three hours after the battle started the English were still standing firm.

Starting positions at the Battle of Hastings

To London

HAROLD

ENGLISH

FRENCH

To Hastings

WILLIAM

0   500 m

- **English**
- **·** Norman archers
- Norman infantry
- Norman cavalry
- **⊠** Base camps

A critical moment

Suddenly the Norman front broke on the left. Men fled downhill. Word spread: 'William is dead!' The Normans were on the run. The English right broke ranks to chase the fleeing enemy. William saw the danger – and the opportunity. He lifted his helmet to show he was alive, then led his cavalry against the English who had left the safety of the shield wall. They were easily cut down. But the English still held the ridge.

The battle in the balance

William had no choice but to go on attacking uphill. Then we think that William ordered his cavalry to charge the English, turn suddenly, pretending to flee, then turn again to cut down those foolish enough to chase them. Even after this the English still had enough men to hold the ridge. By afternoon, many Norman horses were dead or exhausted. Their tired riders had to fight on foot.

The end

Finally gaps appeared in the English line. The Normans pressed fiercely at the centre, towards Harold and his **bodyguard**. Norman archers fired arrows which found more and more targets as the English shield wall broke up. We do not know for sure how Harold died. One story says an arrow hit Harold in the eye, penetrating his brain. However he died, his death marked the end for the English. His bodyguard fought bitterly on, but what was left of the rest of his army scattered as night fell. William had won.

Harold is killed. He is the figure on the right reaching for his eye. Notice the dragon banner and the bodies being stripped of armour.

A close contest?

The commanders

William, aged 38, brave and strong, had fought his first great battle at 19. But Hastings was only his second big battle and the first time he had ever been in command.

Harold, aged 45, had fought successfully against Welsh raiders in 1062–3. His recent victory at Stamford Bridge would have made him feel even more confident.

The armies

Most Normans were fighting out of loyalty to William or in hope of winning English lands. There were also some paid **mercenaries**. The Normans had about 7500 men – 4000 **infantry**, 2000 **cavalry** and 1500 archers.

The English army of 8000 were mostly local men with a duty to defend the country against attack. Some were well-equipped lords, but most were peasants armed only with farm tools and knives. About 800 were from Harold's personal **bodyguard**, experienced and well-armed fighters.

Norman horses fall to the Saxon axe

The core of the battle – mounted Norman knights against Saxon heavy infantry

Tactics

The English blocked the road to London and forced the Normans to fight uphill. This made their cavalry and archers less effective. But the English had no archers or cavalry there. They could only stand firm under repeated Norman attacks.

William had to control three kinds of troops and organize their different methods of fighting so that they supported each other. If he lost the battle, he would lose the **invasion**. He would have to go back to Normandy.

If Harold lost the battle, he could retreat and then raise another army from the west of England.

Win or lose?

William might have lost when his men fled thinking he had been killed. Instead he turned this to his advantage. The deaths of Harold and his two brothers in the battle meant the English had no clear leader after their defeat.

EQUIPMENT

Experienced soldiers on both sides had the same armour – a coat of iron rings or plates, an iron helmet and a shield. Their weapons included swords, spears and maces.

Three major differences were :
- The Norman horsemen had long, heavy spears to charge fixed positions or to kill men running away
- The Normans had many more archers than the English
- The English used small axes for throwing and large ones for fighting hand-to-hand. A single blow from a full-sized battle-axe could fell a horse and rider.

From conquest to crown?

What happened to the dead?

Harold's body was taken to William's camp, then handed over for burial at Waltham Abbey, Essex. The Normans allowed local people to take away any English dead they knew and left the rest to rot where they lay. William let his men rest for five days. Then he set out for London. He had won the battle and killed his rival, Harold. But would the English accept him as king?

The march inland

William used force when he had to, but avoided it where possible. He wanted to save casualties on his side and make a name for himself as hard but fair. The

Norman soldiers burn a house.

people of Romney killed the crews of two Norman ships which had been swept off course. So William attacked Romney to punish them. But when some Normans set fire to houses in Dover after it had surrendered William paid **compensation**.

The Normans were delayed at Dover for a week because many of their men were sick. Finally William marched to Canterbury, headquarters of the English church and capital of Kent. Its leaders came out to surrender, even before he arrived. William stayed four weeks before moving on. He, too, had fallen ill and needed to be fit before marching on London.

Ready for London?

London was England's biggest, richest city. It had strong walls and its own local army. William decided against a full attack. He sent a raiding party which beat back Londoners who came out to fight them. The Normans then burned down Southwark, (outside the city walls) before rejoining William's main army, which had moved on westwards.

Winchester, capital of Wessex, surrendered. So did the ports of Chichester and Portsmouth. William pressed on, punishing resistance with fire and sword. The earls who might have led resistance in London began to squabble among themselves.

William then swung north, aiming to make a ring of conquests around London, before marching on London itself. When he reached Berkhampstead, Hertfordshire, the surviving English leaders came to offer their loyalty. After a march of over 500 km, William finally entered London without a fight and was crowned king in Westminster Abbey on Christmas Day 1066. Once again, his usual mixture of determination and caution had paid off.

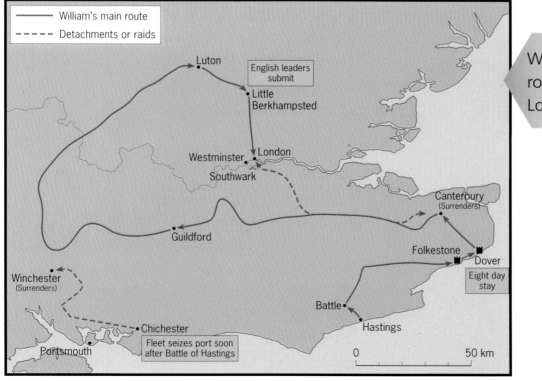

William's route to London

Castles for conquerors

The Normans had England. But they only had about 10,000 men. How could they control over 1,500,000 English people? They needed a way of keeping safe while making sure of their control. Luckily they had just developed one – the castle.

Cheap, quick and easy

People had often built walls and ditches around their towns to defend them. But castles were something new. The Normans used them as long-term homes, as well as for protection against local people. William's **invasion** fleet brought the parts to make a wooden castle with them. So their first castle at Hastings was put up in a few days. As the Normans took over more and more land, they built castles as they went, and put soldiers in them to show the English who was now in charge.

Mottes and baileys

These castles had a mound (motte) made by digging a round ditch and throwing the earth into the middle. On top was a wooden tower (the keep), with a wooden fence round it. The motte was the main strongpoint of the castle's defence.

Norman soldiers put up a prefabricated fort at Hastings.

To get to it an attacker would have to charge across a ditch, often filled with water from a diverted stream, and then up a steep hill. Then he would have to get over a wooden wall into an area in front of the motte, called the **bailey**. This held stables, storehouses and other everyday buildings. Finally the attacker would need to charge up the motte itself, cross its wall and then attack the keep. All the time the defenders would have the advantage of firing down arrows, rocks and spears.

A motte-and-bailey castle could be made from wood and earth in about two weeks. A disciplined army with well-organized supplies could, over time, burn or batter down a castle, or simply starve it out. But a mob of rebellious villagers would be powerless against it.

A motte-and-bailey castle

Wood into stone

As the earth of the motte settled to make a firm base, wooden fences and buildings were replaced by stone walls and towers. William I set the example by building massive stone towers like the Tower of London, and similar strong points a day's march away, at Windsor and Rochester. Later he built stone castles wherever there had been a rebellion, as at Exeter and York.

Resistance

Annual rebellions

By February 1067, William felt secure enough to return to Normandy. But rebellions broke out against Norman rule every year from 1067 to 1070. Most of the risings took place on the edges of areas controlled by the Normans, especially close to Scotland and Wales, where support could be brought in from outside. But the rebels never managed to find a single leader, or organize a nationwide rising.

In 1067, a rising in Kent encouraged Eustace of Boulogne, who had fought for William at Hastings, to besiege Dover Castle. It held out; he retired; the rising was crushed. An attack on Hereford, launched from Wales, was also defeated. In 1068, Exeter rose and held out for eighteen days. It was then allowed to surrender in return for a fine.

The greatest challenge

In 1069, an English rising at Durham wiped out the local Normans. The King of Denmark was invited to send a fleet to support the rebels. Together they took York. Small, local risings broke out from Lincolnshire to Cornwall. But the Norman network of castles held firm. William paid the Danes to go away. Then he turned on his rebellious subjects.

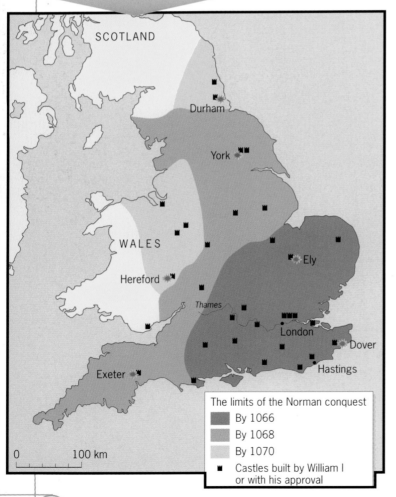

Resistance and rebellion, 1066-70

SCOTLAND

Durham

York

WALES

Ely

Hereford

Thames

London

Dover

Hastings

Exeter

0   100 km

The limits of the Norman conquest
- By 1066
- By 1068
- By 1070
- ■ Castles built by William I or with his approval

The harrying of the north

Small parties of heavily-armed Normans spread out over the countryside, as far west as Cheshire, and as far south as Derbyshire. They burned, looted and slaughtered their way through a great arc of territory. Tens of thousands died. Even more died later from starvation. No invader from Scotland or Scandinavia would be able to live off the land in that territory for years.

The last stronghold

In 1070, supported again by Danes, a final band of resisters joined together in the Fen country around Ely under a lord called Hereward. The dense marshes made it difficult for the Normans' heavy **cavalry** to hunt down Saxons making hit-and-run raids. But the Normans patiently built a firm causeway so that they could ride right into Hereward's stronghold. He escaped, but without his leadership the last resistance ended.

The kingdom secured

In 1072, William led an expedition against Malcolm II of Scotland, who had supported English rebel leaders. He now submitted to William, handing over a son as a **hostage**. In 1075, the Norman lords of Hereford and East Anglia joined an English lord, Waltheof, in rebellion but this, too, was easily put down. William felt safe enough to spend most of his later years back in Normandy.

Village

Main area of revolt in the north

0   100 km

The harrying of the north – villages recorded as still waste in 1086

The take-over

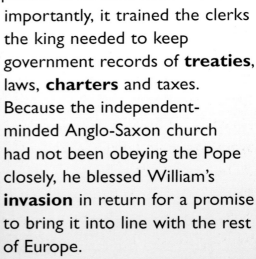

Land

William promised to reward followers by giving them lands. He took the land from the Saxon lords defeated at Hastings and in later revolts. By the end of William's reign most of England was owned by the king himself and 200 of his followers. Only two Saxons remained great landowners and all the Saxons together held only one-twelfth of England's farmland. The rest was held by church leaders and **monasteries**.

Durham – a Norman cathedral. Notice the rounded arches, massive columns and bold geometric carving and decoration.

The Church

The Church not only controlled the nation's religious life, but also about a quarter of all land. Even more importantly, it trained the clerks the king needed to keep government records of **treaties**, laws, **charters** and taxes. Because the independent-minded Anglo-Saxon church had not been obeying the Pope closely, he blessed William's **invasion** in return for a promise to bring it into line with the rest of Europe.

This gave William the excuse to appoint Normans, like his half-brother, Odo of Bayeux, to all the high positions in the Church. They began to build great **cathedrals**, like those at Durham, Winchester and St Albans. Twenty years after the conquest only one Saxon **bishop** was left in office.

A Norman banquet. The Normans introduced French words such as fry, boil, roast, sauce, sausage, pastry, dinner and supper.

The language

The Normans spoke French among themselves, and used Latin for government records. Ordinary people still spoke Anglo-Saxon, the ancestor of English. By about 1400, English was again the main language for everyone, although many nobles and churchmen spoke French, too. Many French and Latin words had become part of English, especially in areas of life controlled by Normans:

- Warfare: *arms, battle, castle, lance, sergeant*
- Government: *council, exchequer, mayor, minister, parliament, prince*
- Law: *arrest, assault, burglary, constable, court, crime, fine, judge, pardon, prisoner, robbery*
- Business: *agreement, bill, debt, money, property, purchase*
- Religion: *chapel, miracle, pray, saint, sermon*
- Architecture: *arch, aisle, column, pillar, porch*

THE HIGH LIFE

The fact that the Normans lived better than Saxons is reflected in the French origin of such words as: *banquet, cards, costume, dice, gown, jewel, lace, leisure, luxury, satin, sport,* and in the fact that animals kept their English names when alive but became French when cooked: *beef, mutton, pork, venison.* Similarly jobs which involved little contact with Normans remained English: baker, fisherman, miller, shepherd, weaver, whereas those that did became French: *butcher, mason, painter, tailor.*

How it happened - the Norman version

A misleading name

Some time before 1083 William's half-brother, Odo, had the *Bayeux Tapestry* made to tell the story of the Norman conquest. It is named after Bayeux **cathedral** in Normandy, where it hung for centuries. It was made in England and is not really a **tapestry**, but an **embroidery**, 50 cm wide and over 100 metres long. It was made by English nuns, probably from the famous needlework school at Canterbury.

Missing meanings

The *Bayeux Tapestry* is a huge strip cartoon. It stops rather suddenly after the battle of Hastings. This may mean a final section is missing, perhaps showing William being crowned.

A Latin text runs along the top, but the pictures are mostly left to speak for themselves. This means that some incidents can no longer be explained. In one section, Norman soldiers are shown hurrying to build a fort, and two of them are shown fighting one another with clubs, but there is no explanation why.

Edward's body is carried to his new abbey church at Westminster. Notice the blessing hand of God.

The story and its purpose

The tapestry uses almost as much space re-telling events leading up to the conquest as on the conquest itself. It shows Harold fighting with William to put down a rebellion in Brittany. It also shows him swearing a solemn oath to support William's claim to the English throne. The tapestry was probably made not only to celebrate the Normans' success in battle, but also to justify the **invasion** by showing that they were in the right. Harold is not, however, shown as a villain, but as a brave leader who has done a bad thing. According to the Norman version he had broken his word and been punished by God for doing so.

Harold swears on holy relics that William will be king of England on Edward's death.

A priceless treasure

The *Bayeux Tapestry* is remarkable because few things as fragile as cloth – easily destroyed by fire, insects or damp – have survived for nine centuries. It is valuable to historians for its vivid pictures of kings and castles, banquets and battles. It also shows what the people of the day felt about these great events and how they thought they should be understood.

The Conqueror's kingdom

The King's order

At Christmas 1085, William I ordered a complete survey of his kingdom. He wanted to know exactly what lands, villages and towns were in his kingdom, what each owed him in taxes and how many soldiers he could raise if he went to war. Castles, church lands, London, Winchester and Northumbria were left out. William already knew about his castles. Church property did not pay taxes. Powerful London was always a special case. Winchester, headquarters for the survey, was a royal centre anyway. Sprawling, lawless Northumbria was remote from royal control.

A page from the *Domesday Book*, showing the King's own lands in Wiltshire.

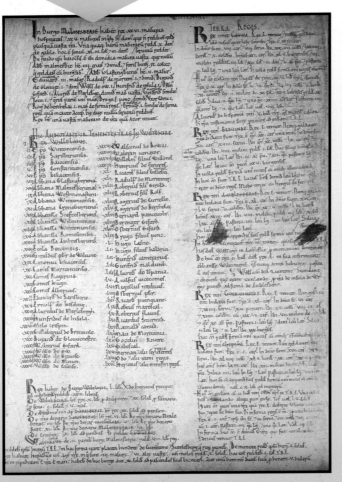

The survey

Clerks rode all over the country to ask the people who ran each lord's land a standard list of questions – the name of the estate; its size; its owner; how many plough-teams of oxen it had; how much woodland, meadow and pasture; how many mills, fisheries or vineyards; how many men – free and unfree; how much livestock; and finally its value in 1066, its value when it was given to its owner and its value in 1086. The questions were asked and answered in Anglo-Saxon, but written down in Latin by scribes who mostly spoke French.

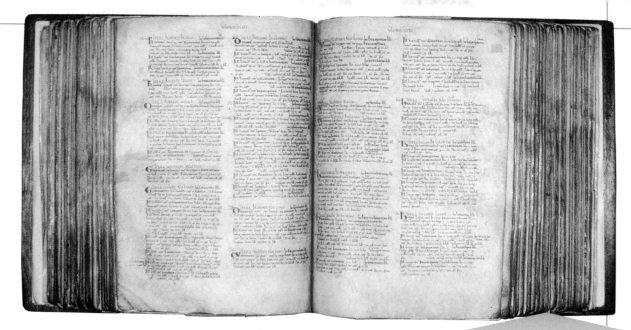

Domesday

The survey took just one year to complete. William died in 1087, so there might have been plans to add the areas originally omitted from the survey. The survey was called the *Book of Winchester*, but it soon got the nickname the *Domesday Book*. It reminded people of the accounting of the Day of Judgment, when the world would come to an end. No other European country ever produced such a detailed record in the Middle Ages and it remained a basic source of information for English governments for centuries.

The *Domesday Book* was a detailed account of the Conqueror's kingdom in 1086.

DOMESDAY ENGLAND

What does the *Domesday Book* tell us?

- William's kingdom was overwhelmingly rural. London, with 50,000 people, was the only real city, ten times larger than the next biggest towns – Bristol, Norwich, Exeter, York, Coventry or Thetford.
- Most of England was farmland or land set aside for the king's hunting.
- In many areas the Book simply said (almost twenty years after the 'harrying of the north'), *'vasta est'*, Latin for 'it is waste'. An Anglo-Saxon chronicler was quite correct when he wrote of William: *'He was very hard and violent, so that no one dared to do anything against his will.'*

Time-line

973	Edgar crowned king of all England
975	Edgar dies; his son Edward succeeds him as king
978	Edward is murdered; his brother Ethelred succeeds him as king
1016	Ethelred dies; his son Edmund succeeds him but dies the same year. Canute becomes king
1035	Canute dies; his sons Harold Harefoot and Harthacanute succeed him
1042	Harthacanute dies; Edward the Confessor becomes king
1049	Edward the Confessor exiles Godwin and his sons
1051	Godwin and his sons regain their lands and power
1062–3	Harold Godwinson and Tostig defeat the Welsh
1064	Harold Godwinson visits Normandy
1065	Tostig is sent into exile. Westminster Abbey is finished
1066	January – Edward the Confessor dies; Harold Godwinson takes the throne of England
	May – Tostig begins raiding the English coast
	September – Harold's fleet and army give up watching the English Channel
	Harald Hardrada and Tostig defeat the English at Fulford Gate
	Harold Godwinson defeats Hardrada and Tostig at Stamford Bridge
	William of Normandy's invasion fleet lands at Pevensey, Sussex
	October – Harold learns of William's landing
	Harold arrives back in London
	Harold is defeated and killed in battle outside Hastings
	December – William is crowned king in Westminster Abbey
1067	William returns to Normandy. Dover castle and Hereford are attacked by rebels
1068	English rising in Exeter
1069	English rising in Durham is followed by the harrying of the north
1070	Hereward's resistance in Ely is ended
1072	Malcolm II of Scotland stops helping English rebels
1075	Last major uprising against William is put down
1086	*Domesday Book* is compiled
1087	William dies

Glossary

besiege	to surround a castle or town to starve it into surrendering or take it by attack
bishop	senior priest in charge of a diocese
bodyguard	unit of professional troops who protect a leader
cathedral	large church serving as a bishop's headquarters
cavalry	troops who fight on horseback
charter	legal document granting a right, to hold land or a market for example
chronicler	recorder of historic events
compensation	money paid to make up for damage or an offence
diocese	area of territory into which a country is divided for church purposes
embroidery	cloth picture made by sewing coloured shapes onto a backing sheet
exile	being forced to live outside one's own country
hostage	prisoner held to guarantee the good behaviour of another person
infantry	troops who fight on foot
invasion	armed expedition into another country, usually to take it over by force
mercenary	soldier who fights for anyone who will pay him
monastery	community of monks
nunnery	community of nuns
tactics	methods of fighting
tapestry	cloth picture made by weaving coloured threads
treachery	betray trust, especially by deserting leader
treaty	formal agreement, often between countries

Index